A WAY FORWARD

AUSTIN CHUCKWUEMEKA KONKWO

ISBN 978-1-7361332-0-0 (paperback)

Copyright © 2020 by Austin Chuckwuemeka Konkwo

All rights reserved. No part of this publication may be reproduced, distributed, or transmitted in any form or by any means, including photocopying, recording, or other electronic or mechanical methods without the prior written permission of the publisher.

CHAPTER ONE

Okoro Oba can still recall events; how they came, how he was able to overcome some of them and how some of them inadvertently came to defeat him. Such is life. When he was about twenty years of age, the ambitious and hardworking man planned great for his future.

Born of illiterate parents, the need for a sound education for him was not given attention. Besides, the only primary school then was inUzuha, which was about fivekilometres from his village Iboko in Umuele community. The trouble of getting to Uzuha from Iboko on a daily basis was much and only for those who could undertake the task and trouble.

In fact, the white man's education in schools then was mostly for stubborn children who could not be controlled by their parents or wards. In such cases, schools were avenues for disciplining them. Also, such was for weaklings who could not use their knives, cutlasses and hoes to farm and feed themselves properly. To such people, schools were where they could go to and serve the white people and feed from the strangers.

To many, the white man's education was a way of losing the much-desired man labour at the farmlands. Such was also for the children of poor people who may not have much food and drinks at home to preside over, occupy themselves with and make merry. For such children of poor people, schools were avenues where they could go to and serve the whites and in the process have food to eat. For many children of the poor, the white man's school was an avenue to go to and seek social and economic cover.

Many of those from noble homes only presided over bulky foods, meat, drinks and lavish ceremonies. To many of such people, the white man's education was an embarrassment, a useless exercise, a nuisance, a threat to their lives and future and need not be cared for. In fact, many saw the act as "an exercise in futility" and "a distraction".

During those days, Okoro Oba had a cocoa plantation which he inherited from his father who died when he was a young boy. His father had told him before he died that the plantation belonged to him. Okoro had seen his parents work on the plantation several times, which made him believe his father then.

After the death of Okoro's father, their town's man, Jabo came to them and appealed to take charge of the plantation for economic use. Those were in the good old days when people saw gold and matched on it; without minding its worth. That was when greed and the love of money was not reigning and was not placed in the prime. Readily the plantation was given out without much questions. No agreement of any sort was called for as may have been the case. The only agreement between the two parties was understanding based on trust; thus, use and give back when required.

The monkey says that why it always carry its young ones carefully at its back is to safeguard and always identify them as most young monkeys look alike". Okoro and his mother did not know that the monkey's belief could become a reality. They never knew that their plantation could become their townsman's property in future.

When Okoro grew to adulthood he requested his plantation for use. But the occupant, Jabo, blatantly refused to surrender it claiming that the plantation rather belonged to him; and no one else. That was because of the immense economic benefits he was deriving from the viable plantation.

After several deliberations to claim back his plantation and there seemed no positive response from the occupant, Okoro invited the elders of Iboko and Umuele in general to mediate and resolve the matter. At the mediation talk, almost the entire elders of Iboko and Umuele in general asked Jabo to surrender the plantation to the owner, Okoro.

Only one man, Gbado, objected to the collective decision claiming that the person using the plantation was rather the rightful owner. This was, because Jabo had given Gbado a life goat the previous day to speak in his favour. Jabo, on hearing that the case with him and Okoro was to be judged had taken many things in the form of gratification to some elders for help. Those he tried to give the gifts objected. Only Gbado received things from him. With Gbado's support, Jabo decided to keep hold of Okoro's plantation.

At themeeting, the elders gave Jabo order to abide by their decision or have a showdown from the entire community.

After the judgement, people departed to theirrespective homes. Gbado also left for his home with others. As he was going, he hit his leg on a stone and bled to death after a short while. Thereafter his remains was hurriedly interred in a forest as the cause of his death was questionable and suspicious. That was the custom at Umuele then.

Jabo refused to yield to appeals to hand over Okoro's plantation to him. So, the only option for Okoro was to head to the district court for justice. The elders of Iboko and Okoro reported the matter to the district authority and Jabo was immediately arrested and detained. He was, however, interrogated and after a short time released onbail.

A date was fixed for hearing of the case in the community's district court. Before the datefor the hearing of the case, Jabosent to the court interpreter two goats and thirty tubers of yam as bribe to enable the interpreter assist him to winthe case.

On the day of hearing of the case, the elders were invited to the court by the village head. Each person, as normal, stood behind the person he or she was siding. Everybody stood on the side of Okoro except Gbado's wife whose late husband had earlier sided Jabo.

There at the court, it was only the District Officer (D.O.) and the Court Interpreter that could speak and understand English language. No other person was literate enough to understand the white man's language.

When the case came up for hearing, the District Officer asked the Interpreter to ask those who were siding the two concerned people the rightful owner of the disputed plantation.

When the Interpreter asked the question almost everyone shouted "Okoro Oba" meaning that Okoro Oba owns the plantation. The majority in the court further pointed at Okoro Oba to further buttress their point. But the interpreter told the District Officer that Okoro Oba was not the owner as the entire people are shouting and pointing against him. Also, when some of the elders volunteered themselves and spoke the truth at the court by narrating the story of the ownership of the plantation from start to the present then, the interpreter interpreted negatively in favour of Jabo.

The District Officer further requested for the site of the plantation. When everybody left for the site of the plantation, the District Officer discovered that the plantation was nearer Jabo's house than Okoro's house. However, the District Officer adjourned the case two days from that day.

On the adjourned date of the case, the District Officer gave judgement in favour of Jabo and gave him ownership of the plantation. He further instructed that Okoro be jailed for a year or pay a fine of one pound in the alternative.

After the judgement, Okoro's mother wept bitterly at the court while Okoro looked helpless. There was confusion by majority at the court.

Okoro was handcuffed by the court police after the judgement. He was about to be whisked off to the prison if not that his mother paid on the spot the one pound fine on him. On receipt of the one pound fine, Okoro was allowed his freedom by the court.

The elders of Iboko after the court verdict announced the ostracization of Jabo and Gbado's wife from their village. That was because they smelt foul play on the part of Jabo as a reason for his court victory. When Jabo heard of the decision of his people, he quickly ran to the interpreter and relayed the decision of his people to him.

The interpreter passed the information to the District Officer (D.O) who ordered the arrest of Iboko people present at the court. With the order, the court policemen immediately moved to effect the arrest of Iboko people present at the court.

As the court policemen were about to arrest them, the leader of the people of Iboko, Okimi, pleaded for mercy. He claimed that they never said that Jabo was to be ostracized from their community. He stated that Jabo was part and parcel of them and has all the privilege and rights of every member of the community.

With Okimi's new song, the D.O directed that the people of Iboko should not be arrested again but warned that any act of disturbance or denial of the rights of Jabo will be frowned at by the court and perpetrators decisively dealt with.

Later, a little school boy who had been following the court proceedings came to Okoro and relayed to him everything that has been happening on that mater including the bad role played by the interpreter. Hearing all that, Okoro was shocked. He immediately gathered his people to let them hear from the school boy what he heard.

When everybody had gathered, Okoro asked the school boy to address them. After the boy's address, everybody was shocked and the elders went to see the District Officer immediately. But at the District Officer's office, the interpreter did not tell the District Officer that some people wanted to see him. The interpreter simply went inside the District officer's office and came out later. When he came out, he informed Okoro and those with him that the District Officer said that he hasfinished finally with the case. He further said that the District Officer wants them to leave the place immediately otherwise they will be arrested and detained.

With the threat from the interpreter, Okoro and those on his side fearfully and hurriedly left the court premises for their homes. However, Okoro realized that he had been cheatedbecause of Jabo'sdishonesty and his own illiteracy.

Okoro, therefore, resolved to send his children to schoolto learn in order not to witness a similar deprivation of justice in the future. Thereafter, many people on Okoro's side including elders advised Okoro to go home and leave the matter to destiny and fate.

Meanwhile, Okoro had lost his plantation; he had been cheated. Okoro had been treated unjustly. Thereafter, people departed to their respective homes. Jabo rejoiced home while Okoro and those on his side went home angry.

CHAPTER TWO

Okoro Obawas good in wood work and joinery and as such, opted for carpentary work. He was also good in design, making him a force to be reckoned with in his chosen profession.

Soon, after the plantation case, Okoro Oba's carpentry business grew tremendously. Okoro became widely known in his business. His works were second to none and spoke for him.

Later, came the time Okoro won a contract for the construction and delivery of forty desks for their district school. The contract was for the sum of five pounds. That was the price according to the interpreter to the mission priest/headmaster of the school who brought the job to Okoro.

Okoro finished the work on schedule and delivered same. The jobs were good and the mission priest commended Okoro for it. Thereafter, Okoro received the five pounds from the interpreter through whom the school paid.

However, during their community assembly, the headmaster told the audience through another interpreter that out of the fifteen pounds contributed towards the school projects ten pounds was used for building desks for the district school.

This meant that the first interpreter collected ten pounds for the desks and gave Okoro five pounds. That was made possible because during the negotiation on the desks, the interpreter was the only one who was communicating between the headmaster and Okoro. Okoro,because he could not understand the white man's language only accepted what the interpreter told him. In otherwords, Okoro was cheated by five pounds.

After hearing the message, Okoro was shocked, uneasy and dissatisfied. Okoro left the place for his home. At home, he dressed up and after some hours left for the headmaster's house. People who knew that he was annoyed tried to prevent him from going out, but Okoro could not be stopped and he left for the headmaster's house.

On his way, Okoro remembered that he will encounter communication/language problem with the Briton mission teacher. So he quickly went to the nearby village of Umojo where he met a service clerk and relayed the matter to him. The man was sad andtwo of them left for the British man's house. When they got there, the interpreter who gave Okoro the furniture work asked them what they had come for.

Okoro and his friend said nothing, but insisted that they would like to see the headmaster. The interpreter guessedthe men's mission, and asked them to go away, as he claimed, the headmaster could not see them dueto his busy schedule.

As the interpreter was trying to render more explanations, Okoro started shouting and calling the interpreter different bad names. Okoro further pushed the man and the man hit his head on the wall and sustained injuries.

When the teacher heard the noise outside his house he came out to know what was happening. He saw his interpreter in a bad condition and the two men there blinking their eyes. The teacher invited two local policemen outside the gate to arrest the two men while his interpreter was taken to ahospital about six miles away for treatment. Okoro and his friend were later detained.

After two days of treatment, the interpreter recovered and was brought back to his place of work. The two men detained were later granted bail and charged to court for assault. Before charging the matter to court, the interpreter did all he could to prevent the case from going to court but all his plans failed. A saying goes that "every day is for the thief but one day is for the owner of thehouse". This time around, luck had ran out of the interpreter. It was time for him to be unearthed.

When the case came up at the court, Okoro was asked what happened. Okoro spoke through the service clerk. He narrated how the interpreter cheated him by five pounds in the desk business. The District Officer became surprised and unhappy after hearing from Okoro.

The white man not only dismissed the interpreter butordered that he be prosecuted. Okoro was thanked for his bravery and observationbut was reprimanded for fighting.

A Way Forward

The news spread far and near. Okoro was glad to have taught the interpreter a lesson even though he was reprimanded.

Six months later, Okoro and another man were nominated for appointment as tax collectors for their community UmueleOkoro was nominated for his bravery so that he could forcefully collect taxes and rates from people, particularly those that may prove stubborn in paying their taxes or rates. During the interview, which was conducted by the Province Officer, it was noted that Okoro despitehis strength, bravery, hardwork and integrity could not speak even passable English language.

The other young man did not have much to offercompared to Okoro in terms of integrity, bravery, strength and hardwork but had the advantage of speaking a manageable English. Since the tax collector will have dealings with the white men, the chief interviewer who only understands English language had no option than to choose the other young man by name Udamo.

When Okoro heard of the development he did not blame himself but simply accepted defeat because he had considered that shortcoming earlier. But he was unhappy. He then concluded that many bad things had happened and more are likely to happen if the situation is unchecked. He had no otheroption than to look for a solution; as a matter of urgency.

Three thoughts came to Okoro. One was to go to school himself or to marry an educated lady. The other was to marry, have children and send them to school.Since

Okoro hada lot to do at home, he waved the idea of going to school himself. He concluded that he will marry and send his offspring to school or marry an educated lady. That could be the solution to theproblem, Okoro realized.

One day, Okoro called his mother and told her of his intention to marry. His mother sanctioned it. Okoro negotiated with a lady from the neighbouring village of Umuba. The lady was pretty and smart. Both sides accepted the marriage proposal. The lady namedUgo had some level of primary education in her tender age. She could speakEnglishlanguage for she schooled for about three years. She could write readable English.The twofamilies had negotiated but a day to doing the necessary marital rites according to the native law and custom, one thing occurred.

Ugo had gone to the stream to fetch water. There, she saw another lady, Onyoye, who got to the stream after her. When it was Ugo's turn to fetch water, the lady obstructed Ugo from fetching. She claimed that she came earlier than Ugo.There was a noisy argument at the stream between Ugo and Onyoye. Other people testified that Ugo came before Onyoye. Almost everybody at the scene pleaded but Onyoye still paid deaf ears, and wanted to fight Ugo but Ugo being disciplined did not confront Onyoye. The people at the scene eventually helped to save the situation.

But people did not know that Onyoye had a selfish end to satisfy and had made up her mind to insult Ugosaying "you are unfortunate. Look at a young pretty and educated lady like you marrying an illiterate. Don't you feel ashamed? You have devalued your personality".

When Ugo returned home, she cried bitterly for the abuses. She had sleepless nights thinking over the statement "beautiful and educated lady marrying an illiterate". Ugo went to two of her lady friends to seek their opinion on the matter - whether it will be nice or not to marry an illiterate. One encouraged her to continue while the other advised her to discontinue. Ugodid not know what to do. She really loved Okoro but thishandicap of illiteracy became a matter of concern to her.

Later, another man privately came to Ugo soliciting her hand in marriage. The man was a teacher with good academic qualifications. Ugo told the man that she was already considering a man, whom her parents had given their consent to. She asked the teacher to come back and get her final decision in that respect. The man accepted that and both parties scheduled to meet in five days time.

Before the rescheduled day of her meeting with the teacher, Ugo revealed her discussion with the teacher to two of her aunts and three of her friends. An aunt and two friends asked Ugo to withdraw her affair with Okoro. They rather supported her proposed marriage to the teacher. They claimed that Okoro's illiteracy could pose a barrier to her having a blissful and robust marriage.And possibly in her educational pursuit.

Ugo later went to her mother and revealed her intention to marry the teacher. Ugo's mother queried that but later accepted it and promised to inform Ugo's father accordingly. Ugo's parents had earlier objected their daughter's marriage to Okoro as a result of Okoro's illiteracy but refused to be an obstacle intheir daughter's choice.

Ugo's mother told her husband about the recent development and they all accepted that. The following day, a message was sent to Okoro and to members of his family to come for an important discussion two days afterward.

On the proposed date, Ugo's father rose and greeted the entire peoplepresent at the place. He gave them good foods and later addressed them. In his statement,Ugo's father related his daughter's unwillingness to continue with Okoro in marriage. Okoro raised his eyebrow in confusion. On enquiring the cause of the recent development by the eldest man in Okoro'sside, Ugo's father replied that it was the decision of their entire family.

Where such type of thing happened in their native custom, the bridemay be required to repay anything spent officially on her since the initiation of the marriage proposal. When that was mentioned by one of the delegates on Okoro's side, both parties accepted it because itwas often the normal thing with their native law and custom. There,a date was scheduled when everything spent on Ugo by Okoro would be paid back.

Okoro was highly depressed. He looked up and down for help but could not get any. He nearly wept. He went up to see Ugo personally. When he came to her the lady looked uneasy. "So this is what you have done to me" Okoro said. "I am sure you are boiling now, please, come back another day for discussion" Ugo replied.

Some people on from Ugo's side, Ugo and Okoro with some of his people went in privately to weigh the exact cost of the things spent on Ugo. They resolved the matter peacefully and in good time. Ugo's father gave a week's time for therepayment.

Three days later, Okoro came to Ugo to have the special talk which Ugo had promised him. Okoro was received warmly at Ugo's house. Food and palmwine was served him too. He ate and drank satisfactorily. After that, Ugo invited Okoro privately to her mother's apartment. There she told Okoro that she had the intention of continuing her studies and as such would not like to marry before completing her primary school. "Even if I want to marry, I would like to marry a teacher who can help me achieve my goal" Ugosaid.

With the above points mentioned, Okoro saw reasons with Ugo and gave her a go ahead to marry another man. He pledged his total support and continued friendship with Ugo's family. He pledged to serve them wheneverasked to do so. "Let this question of marriage or no marriage not destroy the good relationship between my family and Ugo's family" Okoro said.

In her reply, Ugo promised that she would be ready tohelp get a hardworking and loyal lady for Okoro to marry whenever called upon to do that. Okoro thanked her for the statement anyway. He told Ugo's father not to worry about the refund of the money spent on Ugo. He told Ugo's father that he was going to take care of that personally if his people persist on the refund. Okoro thanked everybody, rose quietly and left for home.

Okoro knew what had gone wrong. Evenwithout being told, he knew that his illiteracy has made him lose Ugo's hand in marriage. He was annoyed even though he did not show it.

When Okoro told his people of his decision to abandon his expenses onUgo, some people accepted that while others objected to it.After some arguments, majority accepted his decision and itwas implemented. For over two months Okoro felt Ugo's shock, but it gradually was taken care of.

Okoro seeing his shortcomings started seeking for a genuine and immediate possible solution. He spent a lot of nights thinking of a possible answer. The only possible solution was still to marry, give birth to children and send them to school. That was the only way to curb the ugly situation. Okoro Oba has been cheated and disappointed due to his illiteracy. More of such is likely to happen if adequate measures are not put in place to address the problem. So, there is need to address the matter as it is believed that "a deaf need not be told that there is danger when the market is on fire".

Later on, Okoro negotiated for a wife from yet another neighbouring village, Ubi. For it is said that "if you try and do not succeed keep on trying and never lose hope, for with determination you could realise your aim". Actually "it takes much to become a man".

Okoro never stopped trying and, as a matter of fact, never lost hope. The ladyhe opted for was called Uluma. Both families agreed on the marriage plan. And withoutwasting time and having the commanding power, which is the resources at hand, Okoro applied finishing touches on the lady's marriage rites and finally brought her in under his roof as a wife. That was really great. When both parties started living together, Okoro found out that the lady was actually meant for him and him for her. Okoro came to believe that "when one door closes another opens". Okoro came to realize that the lady was his destined partner despite all odds. He came to know that past attempts to marry was not his destiny.

CHAPTER THREE

Okoro Oba grew from strength to strength and from one achievement to the other. He was an active farmer and not only a carpenter but a highly successful one. After a little time, Okoro'swife gave birth to a baby boy. They named himUchechukwu or Uche in short. They handled the little child with care. Okoro believed that Uchechukwu will be the pillar of his house. Okoro and his wife nursed Uche very well and made sure he grew up in strength and health. Okoro believed that Uche will challenge any shortcoming on his side.

When Okoro and his wife saw their little child somehow grown up, they gave a serious thought over the child's future. One adage says that "whosoever does not think of tomorrow does not feel the impact of the night". For it is at the night when people sleep that they think more of issues that concern them. That is to say that without night for sleep, there may not be much thoughts for tomorrow.

Okoro used to feel the impact of the night and as such thought of his problems. Okoro feeling his bitter experiences in the past vowed to conquer any similar occurrence in the future.

One night, Okoro thought of Uchechukwu and his education. He told his wife about the child going to school and both agreed on the matter. Uluma reluctantly agreed somehow because of the child's tender age. After some discussions, they agreed on the matter.

The following day, Okoro and his wife went to the village new school to enroll Uchechukwu into the school. After a little interview with Uchechukwu, the headmaster accepted enrolling him. To assesshis educational ability, the headmaster asked Uchechukwu some questions in their local languagethus "what is your name?"."my name is UchechukwuOkoro", Uchechukwu replied. "what are the names of your parents?""The names of my parents are Okoro Oba and Uluma Oba", Uchechukwu replied.

The headmaster asked Uchechukwu the name of his village and Uchechukwu smartly replied, "the name of my village is Ibokoin Umuele". The headmaster asked Uchechukwu why he wanted to go to school and Uchechukwu replied that he wanted to go to school to get good knowledge and education. Uchechukwu's parents and the headmaster were impressed.

The headmaster promised enrolling Uchechukwu into the school but told Okoro and his wife that he will do that by January the following year when the new academic year would start. Before concluding on the matter, the headmaster asked Okoro the ageof his child. Okoro after some little calculation said "he is seven years of age". The headmaster to be sure of the matter requested that the young boy should use his right hand to touch his left ear. That was done successfully.

It is said that "a chick that was born during the rainy season, that has chosen to live will certainly withstand the hardship of the season, while that that has decided to die willdie despite favourable conditions". Okoro wants Uchechukwu to be the pillar of their family and has started to lay the solid foundation at the right time. He has taken the right steps and everything seems to be working out despite any odds or circumstances.Uchechukwu and Okoro seem to be succeeding from every angle and from all indications despite perceived shortcomings.

Before the month of January when the new session was to start off, Okoro and Uluma had purchased for Uchechukwu three pairs of white khaki shorts and two white shirts. The clothes were thick and made from salt bags. When January finally came, the couple went to the headmaster for Uche's enrolment. The headmaster took five shillings enrolment fee from Uche's parents and enrolled their child.

"Whoever wants help from people must show the help he has rendered to himself" an adage says. So Uche had been doing and behaving well at home and other places to justify the move to enroll him in school. When Uche enrolled into the school, he gave his studies serious attention. He never missed classes and attendance at school. He never took things for granted. He actually worked hard for everything good. He learned fast. At the beginning of his first year in school, Uche had further learnt a lot of folktales among other stories.

But in his first two months in school, there was a case where a boy came late to school. The boy was penalized by being flogged two strokes of the cane. Observing that, Uche took his bag and ran home for fear of being flogged himself. On getting home, he told his mother what happened. He told his mother that he will not go to school again for fear of being flogged. His mother pleaded with him and promised to accompany him to school the following morning to speak on his behalf.

The following day, Uluma Oba accompanied Uche to school. On getting to the school compound, Uluma went to the headmaster to plead and speak on Uche's behalf. The headmaster saw reasons with her and told Uluma that Uche being a good boy has nothing to fear. He said "I do not think Uche can indulge in a bad practice that will earn him any punishment". He told Uche to keep coming to school in time, read hard and be obedient. Thereafter Ulumaleft and left Uche in school.

CHAPTER FOUR

In his third year in school, Uche won two scholarships. The first scholarship came to him as the best-behaved student in the school. The scholarship was awarded by the mission priest. Uche also won a scholarship as the best footballer in the junior team in his school. The scholarship was given by the District Officer (D.O) of their division. The scholarship covered only tuition fees.

Uche always helped his people at home especially in domestic matters. He also recorded minutes of meeting in English language for his people. With his good idea ofEnglish language, he did not allow cheating at meetings. He wrote agreements for his people and did private things for people without seeking rewards. Whenever his father had issues that had to do with communication in English, he never missed to take Uche along.

Uche participated in village activities very well. He had a kinsman by name Okechukwu, often called Okey. Two of them participated in mice hunting very well. Okechukwu was older than Uche. Whenever they went for the exercise, they used to catch a good number of mice and often squirrels. Whenever Uche caught any of these, he handed themover to Okechukwu, who in turn prepared same for food. Whenever Uche killed anything he simply waited for Okechukwu to come and take the animal and prepare same for food by roasting.That was because Uche did not know much about animal roasting.

There was a time when Okechukwuwas sick. Uche killed some mice but could not roast them, becauseOkechukwucould not render any help.The animals spoiled and were thrown away. When Uche told Okechukwu of the incident, he was displeased.

This made Uche to seek a way out over that.Uche went to Okechukwu to ask him how to prepare animals for consumption. Okechukwu readily rendered help. He told Uche that the only way to do itis to put the animal into a fire, leave it for sometime so that the hair couldgo off. Use a knife to remove the burnt hair, remove the intestine and every other thing inside the stomach; wash it, add raw oil, pepper and salt inside the empty stomach and roast it with fire. Uche being a fast learner learnt immediately.

The following day, Uche went for a mice hunt in the evening. He succeeded in catching two big mice. On getting home, Uche simply prepared fire with firewood, put the two mice inside the fire and allowed their hair to go off through burning.

When their hair had gone off, Uche used his knife to cut the stomach of the animals. He removed their intestines and its contents. He washed them and added some salt, pepper and raw oil inside their stomach and finally kept them at the fish cage to roast for a day. When Uche came to taste the meat, he found out that it was even sweeter than those Okechukwu had been preparing. From that time, Uche mastered the job and became an expert in mice roasting.

Whenever Uche's younger brothers caught rats or mice, they brought them to him to prepare in the special way. That, Uche did with keen interest and excellentlytoo.

Also Okechukwu being a kinsman to Uche lived symbiotically with him. They both shared their pleasures and sorrows. Okechukwuand Uche brought pears which they used to eat together. When Okechukwu's family pears finished, a thought came to him and that was to pluck the pears of those of theirneighbouring villagers. He told Uche how they performed the deal.

Okechukwu told Uche that they should climb the pear tree, pluck many fruits, keep it in a bag with them on the tree. If the owner comes, they should leave the bag to fall with a heavy noise. In that process, the owner hearing the noisecould run away thinking that the plucker had fallen off, and may have sustained injuries. Thereafter, they will climb down, carry their bag and run away. When Okey told Uche that, Uche refused following him. Hehad not done such a deceit before and as such did not know much about it. After much pressure from Okey, Uche agreed tofollow him for the first time. It is said that "when a goat thatdoes not chew cud follows that which chews cud it could start chewing cud". Uche associating with Okechukwu had decided to follow Okechukwu in that act. They agreed to perform the deal at a pear tree near their village.

When the boys realised that people had gone out for their normal businesses, they took off for the activity. They usedtwo bags for the deal. When Okechukwu climbed up, he askedUche to watch out when someone would be coming. When Okeyhad plucked a good number of pears, the boys were seen by two people. The first was a woman who was going to her farm. When she came to the scene, she saw Uche down andOkey up a pear tree. The womansaw what was happening but pretended as if nothing had gone wrong. She was a good friend to Uche's mother. When the woman asked Uche what he was doing there, Uche replied that he was strolling for sight seeing.The woman did not raise alarm but went away. She did not take action. She rather told Uche to search his conscience, be a good person and never put himself and his family to shame.

The next to come there was a little girl whose father owns the pear tree. She was passing when she saw a person on a branch of the tree. The girl quietly went home and revealed the matter to a man she saw at home. The man came to see things for himself. When he came to the place, Uche immediately ran away whileOkechukwu being clever allowed the bag of pear to fall down.

The noise was so heavy that the man who came therecould not comprehend what happened. So the man ran away. Okechukwuseeing the man running away, cleverly, came down, picked his pear fast bagged it well and ran away with the pear. On reaching home,Okeyrevealed the issue very well to Uche. They congratulated each other for ajob well done.

That evening, the woman that saw Uche at the pear side came to Uche's mother to reveal the secret. She told Uche's mother to stop Uche from relating with Okechukwu. She told Uche's mother that Okechukwu could lead Uche into trouble. She told Uche's mother how Uche and Okechukwu went out to the neighbouring village to steal pear. Although she told the story to Uche's mother privately but Uche seeing the woman knew she had brought a complaint concerning him.

After the complaint, Uche's mother called Uche and asked him what happened. Uche revealed that Okey approached him to execute a deal to steal pears and how he obeyed him. He, however pleaded guilty to the offence saying that, that was his first time. Uche's mother was annoyed. She did not let the matter go far but rather resolved it herself. She told Okechukwu's parents that she will not tolerateOkechukwu's relationship with Uche any longer. She warned Okechukwu personally not toassociate himself with Uche, andalso sternly warned Uche not to relate with Okechukwu again. An adage says that "whatever has a beginning must have an end". That weakened the boys' intimacy and their good relationship eventually broke down.

At home, Uche never liked idleness. He preferred being busy. There was a man who really lovedUche and Uche in turn loved him. The man was namedUkachukwu. He was a craftsman by profession. Uche hadmuch interest in artistic and craft job. The man helped Uche by teaching him the profession and the ethics in it; at his convenience.

Uche in turn, taught the man how to read and write. Their friendship became intimate even though the man was far older than Uche. So, within a space of six months of their relationship, Uche learnt very much in crafts. He used his spare time to do crafts which he presented at school during handiworkprogramme and presentation. He could construct good baskets, mortars and pistols. He even used that to generate income at home. He built a good number of that which his mother sold and got money from.

Uche never missed association with his mates. When youths follow, they interact a lot both in body and in soul. Next to their door was a boy called Onyeha. The young man was an active fisherman. He used nets to catch fishes. There was a day Onyeha made a big catch. He filled his goatskin bag with different types of fishes which he caught. Before he could come back, the news of his big catch had spread far and wide. His mother, sisters and brothers came to embrace him on his way home. They welcomed him warmly.

Uche and his mother were among the spectators. Uluma seeing Uche said "If my child has grown up this is one of those good things I should have been enjoying. My own time is coming", Uche heard all that. When he went in to sleep, Uche thought over his mother's statements and thought over a possible solution. He finally came to the conclusion that to fish and bring a bumper of fish home was the only answer as "impossibility is only found in the hearts of lazy people". Also, an adage says that "whoever says yes to a thing, his creator endorses same for him"

The following evening, Uche picked some of his father's nets and some sticks with hooks for catching fishes and set off with others for a fishing expedition. He caught some insects and dug some worms from the muddy soil at the banks of the rivers as prey for the fishes - to be put on the hooks.

Uche learnt quickly from others that night the tactics of fishing. He put all the hooks with the preys leaving the extreme which will get hold of the fish if it tries to eat the prey. He used his initiative and did a lot that night. When he had set all of the hooks with preys, he quietly set the fishing sticks at strategic positions in the river.

After a little time, Uche heard a noise near one of his sticks. He went to see what the matter was. As he drew near, the noise continued. He was afraid. He ranquickly to inform one of his friends who had come for the fishingwith them. The man was older than Uche.

As two of them drew near, the noise continued. The man gradually lifted the stick. It seized coming out. After applying some force and tricks the stick was brought out with a very big fish. Uche was extremely happy. During that night, Uche made the biggest fish catch among the fishing participants. Before they could get back to the village, the news had spread far and wide. Everybody was surprised because that was Uche's first time of fishing.

On his way home, Uche's parents, brothers, sisters and relations came to welcome him. On seeing her child, Uluma embraced him. The donkey says that "why it always work hard every time is to make sure it lives upto expectations so that whoever said bad of him in the past may say good of him in future". Uche has worked so hard to make his mother say a different thing unlike in his relationship with Okey.

From that time on, Uche became a renowned fisherman. He brought home a good number of fishes whenever on fishing exercise. As such, many people continued to say good of him.

Also, Uche loved drinking palmwine, particularly those that are sugary. His father was a good palmwine tapper. Most nights after meal, members of Okoro's family will wash down their foods with cups of palmwine. Uche was a very good drinker.

There was a time Okoro went out for his carpentary work at a far distant place. He placed a big container for which palmwine would be sourced from a palm tree. Before then, he told a half-brother to keep watch over the wine. When Uche waited patiently for two days without seeing any palmwine to drink, he started thinking within himself what to do.

"Necessity is the mother of invention". Uche came out in the morning with the solution of climbing the palm tree himself to remove the wine and drink. He looked at the palm tree, which to him looked climbable. He immediately started to climb it with a ladder. The ladder could not make him reach the top of the palm tree. On reaching close to the top of the tree, Uche used his hands to climb further.

Uche hooked to one of the dried palm front as a means of support. Unfortunately the palm front was so dry that it fell off. Uche fell down from the palm tree. On getting on the ground, Uche saw the trees and the world going in cyclic direction. He did not know where he was then and what he was doing. Afterstaying for about ten minutes there, he regained consciousness. He came to know what had gone wrong.

He did not sustain much injury. Only a minor one occurred on his knee which hit the ground. He stayed there for another fifteen minutes after which he took his ladder and left for home. On reaching his house, Uche's mother asked him what had gone wrong on his knee and where he had gone with the ladder. Uche replied that he had gone to climb a tree and that is where he sustained the injury. His mother sympathized with him, nursed the injury for him, took care of it until it finally healed.

Uche was also very useful to his parents in economic and social activities. One crucial thing he did at home every morning was to take the goats and sheep to the bush for grazing. He also brought the animals back to the house in the evening. When the animals are back home, Uche gave them water to drink.

Also, Uche opened the roost for the domestic fowls to go out to look for food in the morning. At night he would check the fowls to know whether all have returned or not. If anyone was not seen, he would alert his parents and everyone would search for the missing fowl. Whatever was the case, Uche would close the roost before going to sleep. Uche in fact, did his domestic activities diligently.

Uche did not like to miss tales particulalrly when there was something to wash it down with. During night tales, fires were made in which pears and maize were roasted. As people told tales, they ate roast pear and corn. Other packages that went on with tales included palm wine. Other things that were eaten while tales were told included roast yam, roast fish, roast meat, prepared oil bean fruit among others.

Fires were necessary during tales particularly during cold weather likeharmattanseason. That was to provide warmth to the body. In that case, fires were made and people stayed by its side to heat up their body, tell their tales and eat anything that may be available. People were happy.

CHAPTER FIVE

One day while Uche was going to school, he saw a little bird hopping. He stood attentively and watched it perform. He thought over the incident squarely but could not find the answer. The little bird made some moves towards Uche's axis. Uche wanted to run because his father used to tell him that "when you wake up in the morning and a little bird tries to pursue you, you should run away for you do not know whether it had laid some teeth over the night".

But having a heart of a lion as his father, Uche stood firm. He watched the bird for some seconds. A second thought came to him and that was to catch the bird and use for anything. He sanctioned that and went for the bird. Uche went silently for the bird and quietly caught it. The bird nearly escaped the catch.

Uche was very happy. He did not go to school that day but rather took the bird home. He did so many things for the bird which he tied to a stick. He gave it raw and cooked food to eat and water to drink. He told the bird stories. He tried to teach the bird different things. He danced with the bird. He carried it on his legs and on his chest and still wanted ways to satisfy it the more.

The following day Uche abandoned his school and took care of his august visitor. He never did anything at home be it domestic, educational or manual, but concentrated on attending to his bird. That day, Uche thought the bird was having a hard time with the thread he put on its legs. He observed that when he saw the leg tied by thread to a stick swelling. Uche accepted not to harm the bird any more. After feeding the bird that morning Uche removed the thread on its legs and watched it relax.

The bird observing that the margin between it and the heavens had shortened flew away. It flew far and far, wide and wide and never returned. Uche stood at a point, looked dizzily, helplessly and bitter. Uche linked the cause of the problem to his father's refusal to force him to go to school that day. "If my father had forced me to go to school, I shouldn't have seen or observed that the bird's leg was swelling and I shouldn't have been around to let the bird off the hook. I shouldn't have bothered removing thread from it" Uche stated. Uche waited for the bird to come but it never did.

When his father came home from the day's activities, Uche narrated his sad story to him. Okoro consoled him and realised that despite his educational pursuit, Uche was still adolescent and behaved assuch. Uche had bitter moments over the sad event for some time which later wore away.

After the bird had flown away and Uche had suffered its departure for a little time, he resumed normal activities. He attended school regularly and promptly. He did his domesticand manual jobs very well.

Three days later, Uche saw the bird in a dream. He saw himself using corn to attract the bird. The bird initially showed somewillingness but later objected. After using many tricks to attract the bird which showed no positive response he later used force to catch the bird. He pursued it with forcebut failed to catch it. On his way pursuing the bird, he saw somebody who harassed him by accusing him that he was the person that had been destroying his farm. Uche was greatly surprised. The man attempted to fight him but he ran away for his life. He later woke up and found out that it was all a dream.

Uche had a lot of events during those school days. There was a case in which he ate some oranges with the seeds.

He told one of his colleagues at school that he had eatenorange seeds. His colleague wanted to make him afraid by tellinghim that the orange seed will germinate through his head and people will be climbing it. Uche was greatly worried over that. Within two days that he was thinking over that, he got slim in appearance. He later refused going to school for fear that there may be no life for him when the tree grows on his head.

One morning, Uche told his father that he ate orangeseeds and he was worried over what may be the outcome. His father refuted the claim that a tree will grow on his head. On hearing the right thing, Uche was extremely happy and carried on his duties vigorously. However, that made Okoro to further know that despite Uche's educational pursuit, a child will reason like a child. He had earlier assumed the contrary -that a child will reason and behave like an adult with education.

Uche attended school regularly. At school he never missed listening and comprehending stories. The school had a time for story-telling, and that was Uche's best period at school. Uche could miss any other thing or any other period at school but not story telling period; unless he was not in school.

One day at school, Uche learnt of a legend on why thetortoise has a broken and joined shell. Uche rehearsed thelegend and/waited for the time to go home.

At night after dinner, Uche cleared his throat and asked his parents thus "do you know why the tortoise has a broken and joined shell?" His parents knew where he was trying to arrive at but pretended by saying "no". They knew the story Uche wanted to tell them. They said "no" so that Uche could tell them the story. They also wanted to give Uche a sense of belonging.

Uche started the story thus: "Once upon a time, all animals were invited to the sky for a feast. Tortoise who does not have feathers asked for feathers from other animals to enable him fly and attend the feast in the sky. Other animals obliged and gave tortoise some of their feathers. Tortoise joined the feathers to his shell and started to fly. But before the day of the feast, tortoise cunningly changed his name to 'all of you'. On the day of the feast, tortoise flew to the sky with the help of the feathers which other animals gave him; in the company of other animals. At the feast, food and drinks were served to guests by the host. When tortoise asked the host whom the food and drinks were for, the host said that the food and drink are for 'all of you'. Tortoise immediately collected the food and drink and had them alone because his name was "all ofyou". Other animals were annoyed with tortoise because hewas a cheat. In retaliation, other animals plucked off their feathers from tortoise and left for their respective homes. Tortoise stayed in the sky for many days without food to eat water to drink and without a means to fly back to his home. As such, tortoise suffered in the sky. For the tortoise to come back home,he had to throw himself down from the sky. When tortoise landed on theearth, his shell broke into piece. To have a relief from his crises, tortoise went to a body and bone repairer for treatment. The person cemented the broken shell of tortoise together and he was left with a broken and joined shell."

After the legendary story, Uche's parents were highly excited. They were happy to note that Uche was doing well academically at school. Okoro beat his chest and promised to buy Uche another pair of his school uniform. Uche's mother also promised to buy him the remaining books which he did not have then. Uche further told them some recitations he learnt at school. All the pledges were redeemed the following day.

The new gifts enhanced Uche's interest towards education. He woke up early in the morning before any other person and prepared for domestic work and school. He took his bath early no matter how cold the water could be.

Later, it was time for examinations. Uche put good efforts in the examinations. His mother had promised to roast a fowl for him if he comes first in the class, while his father had promised to buy a pair of sandals for him if he comes first.

Uche eventually came first in the examinations. The news of his success spread throughout Iboko and Umuele. When Uche returned home, his mother redeemed her pledge. She roast a fowl for Uche to eat. Okoro also bought a pair of sandals for him. That was how Uche had a pair of sandals in his primary school. Uche was among the few pupils in his school who had a pair of sandals then. That was how Uche came among the privileged people in his school – for having a pair of sandals.

CHAPTER SIX

At home, Uche helped his people very much in domestic and farm work. After meals, he washed plates. He helped to sweep the rooms and the surroundings. The first room he loved sweeping every morning was his father's room, after which his mother's room followed.

Whatever he learnt in school, Uche came back to implement at home. When Uche learns about hygiene at school, he immediately implements at home. His school which had a period of hygiene and health education taught the pupils the importance of cleaning their teeth and mouth, bathing properly, sweeping and clearing the rooms and its environs among others.

There was a case in which Uche called up his mother, father, brothers and sisters at home and told them of the importance of hygiene. He told them the need for bathing, sweeping the rooms, washing the plates and otheraspects of hygiene. He told them that the first thing somebody should do at home early in the morning is to greet members of his family. Thereafter, the person should clean his mouth with a chewing stick. Other things that may follow include sweeping the house and its environs, cooking, washing utensils, bathing and so on. Members of his family were impressed with the development. On that spot, his father told his mother that as long as he lived, he will never deny Uche any type of education no matter how costly it could be.

As days passed by, Uche grew in soul, body and mind. He did things conscientiously. He was also very good in sports. He was a force to be reckoned with in sports in his school and community. He was good in football and handball. His impact in sports went far and wide. Irrespective of his interest in sports, he never left his studies tosuffer. He maintained both but gave his educational work priority.

During his fifth year in the school, there was a case in which two boys were fighting in the class. Efforts by members of the class helped to save the situation. When tension hadsubsideda bit in the class,and normal business had resumed, one of those involved in the fight threw a piece of stone at his opponent. The stone by mistake came to Uche and hit him seriously atthe back.

Uche felt the pain seriously and was angry. He went to the boy concerned to ask what had gone wrong for him to be involved. Instead of the boy pleading for mercy, the boy rather rendered abuses on Uche. Uche's anger went up and he replied the boy with a slap and beatings. Blood oozed out of the boy's nose and the headmaster and teachers were informed.

Uche became afraid and ran out of the class through the window. The headmaster ordered a chase on Uche and all the members of the class ran after him. All attempts to get hold of Uche proved abortive and they reported that Uche had ran away. The headmaster was annoyed and he decided to go to Uche's home to pick him; in the company of some people.

Before the headmaster set off to look forUchechukwu, he took the wounded boy for first aid treatment in the school. After that, he asked that the boy be taken to the District Medical Centre for treatment. The headmaster and others later left for Uche's house. The headmaster on reaching Okoro'shouse ordered that Uche be picked when they saw him. A boy ran to catch Uche. Uche ran as the boy tried to get hold of him.

On hearing of Uche's trouble at school, Okoro Oba ran from where he went for workto meet Uche at school. On reaching the school, Okoro was told that Uche hadran home. On getting home, Okoro saw the headmaster with some pupils in his house. Okoroasked what had gone wrong. The headmaster did not say anything to the question but instead asked Okoro to look for his son for them.

Okoro again asked the headmaster what had gone wrong but the headmaster did not say anything. Okoro Oba being suspicious of the whole thing and feeling threatened brought out his machete from his room.

On seeing the machete, the headmaster and his team ranaway for their safety. The headmaster ran to the District Officer and reported the matter. The District Officer ordered the police to arrest Okoro. Those delegated came with arms to Okoro's house. The police came in the midst of the village head. On seeing the village head and the police, Okoro surrendered himself to them. They immediately arrested Okoro and locked him up in the district office guard room.

Uchechukwu was arrested later and locked up with his father. After staying a day at the guard room, Okoro and his son were tried at the local court. During the trial, Uchechukwugave his oral statement and the two boys that fought at school gave theirs. The headmaster gave his and finally Okoro was given audience to express himself. Okoro narrated what happened. He claimed that he was provoked hence he acted the way he did to defend himself.

Asked by the District Officer if he was guilty of offence, Okoro said "no". The headmaster became annoyed. He stood up, took permission from the District Officer to challenge that. After being granted permission the headmaster said that Okoro brought out his knife and used it to pursue them. He gave evidence with two witnesses that accompanied him. Asked by the District Officer if the allegations were true or not somebody in the Headmaster's entourage said what he saw.

The persontold the District Officer that Okoro brought out his knife as a means of defence.He said that Okoro did not use the weapon other than for self defence. He said that after watching Okoro grumbling and quarrelling within himself for a little time, the headmaster went to call the police. At that moment they had left the scene for their homes. The District Officer did not mention anything about weapon again.

After a little dialogue between the District Officer and members of his Judicial team, there was a compromise. The District Officer blamed Okoro Oba for bringing out his knife at the incident and emphasized that with the knife Okoro can wound even kill a person if provoked. He also flayed the headmaster's attitude of not listening and responding to Okoro when he intervened. He, however, fined Okoro one pound or to go to prison for six months. After pronouncing the judgment, the policemen handcuffed Okoro to be taken to the prison. On seeing the development Uluma, Okoro's wife cried bitterly.

Later, the District Officer ordered the headmaster to judge the case among the pupils and penalize any of them according to his misdeeds in line with the provisions of the law. He, however, asked the headmaster not to harm the person that testified. He asked the headmaster to consult him if he encounters any difficulty. Thereafter, Uluma brought out one pound and paid her husband's fine and her husband was set free.

At the school, the headmaster suspended the two boys who were involved in the fight for two weeks. He asked them to call their parents who would sign an undertaking for them to be of good behavior on their resumption without which they will not be readmitted. The headmaster told Uche at school that he would be responsible for settling the hospital bill of the student he wounded.

Okoro Oba was somehow happy to have a brave son, Uche. Although, he did not express his happiness before Uche in order not to make him to choose the path of stubbornness but did so to his wife privately. He rather told Uche before his wife, brothers and sisters to always make use of his initiative at very sensitive and delicate moments.

On hearing from Uche that he would be responsible for the hospital bill of Uche's opponent at school, Okoro promised to pay back whatever was the amount to the headmaster. On her side, Uluma begged her son to be careful and obedient in order not to have a repeat of such an incident in future.

Later, Okoro Oba set off to see the headmaster in order to pay the hospital bill of the wounded pupil. On arriving the headmaster's office, he greeted the headmaster humbly. The headmaster reluctantly responded as if he had a nut to crack inside him. Okoro quietly went closer to him and greeted him for the second time.

Okoro further asked of members of his family, work and other things with a free mind. The headmaster responded. After that, Okoro cleared his throat and told the headmaster that he had come for two things. One was to pay the hospital bill of the wounded student and the other was to plead for leniency for what happened the other day, concerning his son Uche.

Both men have been friends for some time. On seeing Okoro's good manner of approach, the headmaster appreciated that. After telling Okoro to sit down he said "welcome my good friend". Okoro humbly sat down.

Okoro pleaded for what happened in the past and claimed that such was the handiwork of the devil. He strongly promised that there won't be any act like that from him again. The headmaster sympathized with Okoro and said that "children must behave like children and when they misbehave an adult should not allow his or her anger to go up as a result of their misbehaviour". The headmaster considering Okoro's manner of approach, Uche's good performance at school and their past state of friendship asked Okoro not to worry about the hospital bill which he personally paid for.

Even with much pressure to repay the hospital bill, the headmaster persistently refused. Thereafter Okoro left for his home.

Two days later, Okoro and his wife met the headmaster with a jar of palm wine at the headmaster's house. They were received by their host. The headmaster served his guests with kolanuts and palmwine. The couples ate and drank together. Thereafter, Okoro cleared his throat and told the headmaster that he had come with his wife who was desirous to see him for the good work he has been doing for her in taking proper care of his son Uche at school. And also for his kindness in shouldering the hospital they would have paid.

In his response, the headmaster said that he quiteappreciated their visit and pleaded that the matter should not go further. He said thatthe past should not tarnish the good relationship between the two families. He said he was surprised to hear that Uche fought with somebody. He said that he believed that Uche was one of the best-behaved pupils he had ever seen. He however said that "if a snake refuses to bite, children may use it as a thread" hence Uche fought when provoked. After that, the couple left for their home.

A saying goes thus, "if someone is going at a narrow path, if his body does not scratch at an object, his cloth could do so". Four days later, Uche went to a stream to fetch water in the midst of others. On getting to the stream, one boy looked at Uche and said, "Uche the trouble maker". Uche got angry and fought the boy and wounded him. He made the boy to sustain injuries on the face, nose andears. The fight extended to Uche's group and the boy's group. If elders had not saved the situation a lot of bad things would have happened.

The news spread round the village and soon Okoro and his wife arrived the scene. The elders did not talk much, but everybody took his or her wardhome. Okoro was afraid and did not know what to do. Okoro wondered if anything had gone wrong with the recent developments. So, the following day, heasked his mother to go to a prophet and seer to enquire if anything had gone wrong.

When Okoro's mother came to a prophet and seer, she gave some money to the man. The man after listening to Okoro's mother and after meditating said "you woman go home, there is nothing wrong with your grandson. He was only acting childishly. Nothing is against any member of your family. The young boy will refrain from childish attitudes with time".

On hearing that, the woman left the prophetand seer with happiness. At home, Okoro's mother rested for a while before she relayed the messages se was told. On hearing the story everybody looked at one another for comments. Nobody made any comment.

At night after supper, Okoro called his mother and wife and toldthem that "there are many ways of killing a bird". That is to say that there are many ways of dealing with a situation. He suggested to them that he was planning to send Uche to his headmaster so that Uche can be attending school from the headmaster's house till he completes his studies at the primary school, which would come up in about a year's time. Neither Okoro's wife nor his mother raised any objection to the suggestion.

The following day, Okoro headed early in the morning for the headmaster's house with his wife. On getting there, he found the headmaster with his family having their breakfast. After exchanging greetings with the headmaster's family, Okoro and his wife got seated. The headmaster's wife rose immediately to prepare food for their visitors.

Understanding what the woman was trying to do, Ulumasaid that they have taken their breakfast and therefore would not like to have any other food. "Don't worryyourself" Uluma concluded. Even with much pressure to eat, Okoro and his wife refused to eat despite the fact that they have not eaten that morning. They did not want to bother anyone.

When the teacher had finished the breakfast with his family, he went inside his bedroom, brought out a big kolanut and an overnight palm wine. All ate the kola and drank the palm wine happily. After that, Okoro cleared his throat and said 'If a single person sees a snake, it will look to him like a python'. It could be better to have training from many angles than from one source at least for wider exposure. Uche may not achieve so much in academics if he stays at his home. As a result of that I am considering sending him to you, the headmaster so that Uche can be attending school from your house at least for academic excellence".

Without any hesitation, the headmaster accepted to have Uche live with him. Thereafter the parties departed. On getting home, Uluma told Uche that they were planning to send him to the headmaster so that he would stay with him till he completed his studies at the primary school. Uche willingly accepted that.

In the evening of that day, Uche's books and clothes were packed in a goatskin bag. Before Uluma accompanied Uche to the headmaster's house the following morning, Okoro advised Uche to be of good behaviour to the headmaster and to members of his family. He advised Uche to refrain from any act that could tarnish his image or bring shame to his family. He told Uche that he was not being sent out to the headmaster as a punitive measure but as a way of improving his education. Summarising, Okoro said that a child wholly brought under the roof of his parents may not be exposed to many aspects of life hencemay somehow be disadvantaged.

While at the headmaster's house, Uche developed fast –mentally, academically, physically, morally and otherwise. He lived harmoniously with members of the headmaster's family. His parents paid him visits at intervals. Uche helped Mr. Nwogu, the headmaster, very much at the farm. Mr. Nwogu in turn treated Uche as his own son. He sent his sons errands together with Uche. Uche also undertook some minor assignments like washing, sweeping and fetching of water there. In fact, everybody enjoyed Uche's stay at Mr. Nwogu's house. Uche loved telling stories and as such spent most nights telling folktales and legends to members of Mr. Nwogu' s family.

In his primary five end of the year examination, Uche came first in his class of fifty six pupils. The news spread far and wide. Within three hours of the release of the results, his parents came to congratulate him at the school. On seeing their son, Uluma embraced him and his father shook him. After the release of the results, cametime for the long vacation. Uche spent almost the entire holiday at Mr. Nwogu's house.

Just about two weeks to reopen school, the headmaster told Uche to go and spendone week with his parents and come back to prepare for the next session with the remaining one week. The headmaster reluctantly released Uche because of the immense use Uche was to him.

While Uche was spending the one week break with his parents, his people took proper care of him. They pampered him as they never did before. His parents had come to see some good developments in their son. They did openly express that before Uche.

During his short stay at home, Uche never missed his hobby of fishing and craft making. When it was time for him to go back to Mr. Nwogu, everybody at home was sad and had wanted him to stay longer with them. But realising that he was going for somethingbetter they obliged him to go.

After a week of resumption in school, Uche registered for the standard six leaving certificate examinations. He read very well throughout that period. Mr. Nwogo directed his family not to bother Uche much with domestic assignments so that he could tackle the assignment ahead of him. He gave Uche moral instruction as often as possible and taught him as much as he could.

Uche grew up with Mr. Nwogu's sons in body and in soul. Mr. Nwogu's son Chika very much resembled Uche. They worked, played and read hand in hand. They were of the same age and of course in the same class.

The boys were enrolled for the standard six Leaving certificate examinations and that of College Entrance Examination when the forms came out. That was done by Mr. Nwogu with financial assistance from Okoro Oba. After a month of the standard six examinations came the College Entrance Examination.

Therewere only five colleges in that part of the region then. The boys (Uche and Chika) waited patiently for their results in the examinations to be released. The standard six examination was marked overseas and it took long for the result to be sent to the concerned people. So, the boys were not in a hurry to have the results. The boys were more anxious of the College Entrance Results to enable them proceed to the secondary school.

CHAPTER SEVEN

After sometime, the result of the College Entrance Examination was released. Mr. Nwogu gave Uche and Chika a good sum of money to travel to the college they applied for admission to check their results. At the college, the boys joined the queue of result checkers and waited patiently for their turn to see their results.

When it got to their turn, Uche was the first to check for his result. The surnames of those that passed the examination was typed alphabetically. When it came to O, Uche did not see his name in the list. He looked through it threetimes but did not see his name.

But Uche was confident of passing the examination. He knew what he wrote and was very sure that he passed. Uche was extremely surprised at the development. Without much argument, he allowed Chika to check his own result. Chika quietly looked through and saw his name. He was happy and he jumped for joy.

Uche insisted on seeing the Principal for the true position of things, for he could not believe his eyes. He went straight to the Principal's office to see things for himself.

On getting there, the typist refused to allow Uche to see the principal even with pressure from Uche. While coming out from his office, the Principal asked Uche if he was looking for him. Uche replied "yes sir". "Come in my son" the principal said. Uche immediately went in. "What is the matter, can I help you?" The Principal questioned. Uche told him that he had come to check his examination result.

The Principal gave Uche paper to write his name. He used the master list he was having and checked for Uche's name. The scores were arranged in a descending order. There, it was observed that Uche came third in the examination. The principal congratulated him for his success. But Uche was surprised on what he heard. He told the principal that he had gone to theperson who was showing the result but was told that he did not pass. He said that he has checked the list of successful candidates but did not see his name.

The principal was surprised. He sent for the person showing the result. On arrival, the principal took the list from the man showing the result. After observing the result, he was surprised that Uche's name did not appear there. He smelt foul play, and asked the man why Uche's name was not on the list. The person told the principal that the typist gave him the list to show to the people concerned and that he did not know anything about it.

The principal sent for the typist. On asking the young typist if he knew anything about the change in the result list, the typist replied "no". The principal was surprised and sent for the police. The police came and arrested the two men.

A Way Forward

After a thorough investigation, it was proved that the typist was responsible for the foul play. Uche was actually among those thatpassed the examination. But the typist at the school neatly erased his name from the list of successful candidates and replaced it with another person's name who allegedly gave the typist bribe to do the evil. He was prosecuted and jailed for six months. After judgment, he was dismissed from work. Uche was, however, offered admission into the school. The admission list was further scrutinized by the Principal.

It must be recalled that at the sad event, Uche and Chika stayed at the College till the typist was tried at the law court. The school housed them till they gave evidence at the court.

When Mr. Nwogu waited for sometimeand could not see his boys, he got worried. He left home for the school. On getting to the school he went straight to the Principal. At the principal's office, Nwogu complained that he sent two of his boys to come and check for their results but has not seen them. Mr. Nwogu complained that he was confused and could not know what to do. When asked of the names of the concerned people, the headmaster replied "Chika Nwogu and Uche Okoro".

Mentioning the names the principal recalled that they were the people he held to help in an investigation. Without wasting time, Mr. John Walker the principal explained to Mr. Nwogu what happened. He told him how Uche passed the examination and how a typist erased his name and replaced it with another name. On hearing the case, he invited a police investigation into the matter and had kept the boys to help in giving evidence. On hearing the news Mr. Nwogu replied,"Oh! thisworld is full of sin". He was completely dejected. When the boys arrived they still relayed the same story.

As time went on, Uche and Chika were given the school prospectus. In the prospectus was stated when the school will reopen, books to be read at the school, and other items likely to be used at the school.

With the news of Uche's admission into the college, there was jubilationin Uche's home. Everybody was happy. When Uche knew that everybody's mind was filled with happiness, also he told his people the dark part of the story. He told them of his bitter experience at the college. How he was nearly robbed of his success and how he ran into luck with the school principal. On hearing the dark side of the story everybody was perplexed. But Uche told them that the typist was sacked.

Later, Okoro invited people in hisvillage to celebrate with him on his son's success. It was jubilation also at Mr. Nwogu's house for Chika.

That evening every elderly member of the town came with a jar of palm wine while the women came with a plate of oil bean fruit. After eating and drinking, Okoro broke the news of his son's success at the College Entrance Examination. The entire community congratulated him and promised to give him individual assistance to help Uche at the school.

During Uche's stay at home, he received handsome material gifts and words of encouragement from members of his community. Those that had no material giftsgave moral support.

After staying for a while at home, Uche went back to Mr. Nwogu to finalize arrangements for his admission into the college.

After a day at Mr. Nwogu's house, a letter came to Uche through his college address that he had been granted a scholarship award by the British Government for coming third in the entrance examination. According to the letter, the scholarship was only awarded to those who had the first, second and third position in the College Entrance Examination at his school. The scholarship covered only tuition fees meaning that Uche's educational burden was fairly relieved in terms of finances.

For Uche's school, his parentsbought five shorts and five white short sleeved shirts for him. All the dresses were made of khaki and sowed by the British tailors at the district mission's office.

Okoro and Ulumaregarded Uche as their only hope on earth. Whatever Uche asked for was provided him. They further bought a wooden box, a pair of leather sandals and a kerosene lamp for him.

Before Uche's departure to his school, his parents called him up one morning to advise him. First to talk was his mother. His mother reemphasized that Uche was the pillar of their family. She told him that they have denied themselves of so many things to see that they train him. She advised Uche to refrain from bad companies that may lead him astray. She pleaded with Uche to be hardworking, and be loyal to his school authorities. She told Uche the evils that may accrue from fighting and advised him to refrain from bad acts.

The advice period lasted for more than an hour, and Okoro persistently told Uche of how he lost many things in life as a result of his illiteracy. He said that why he was struggling to educate him was to make sure that what happened in the past does not repeat itself. He informed Uche that whoever is not educated in future stands the risk of witnessing deprivation of many things. He told Uche to refrain from fighting because the life of indiscriminate fighters is often insecure. He emphasized that Uche is leaving him and his family to a different area to be educated and as such should be careful. He told Uche not to bring shame to his family. He told him to shun bad gangs that can lead one astray. He advised Uche to be watchful over questionable characters and to deny them his association.

Okoro Oba finally asked Uche his son for a response. Uche readily reaffirmed his positive stand by promising to be loyal to the school authorities, to be hardworking, to read his bookswell and refrain from bad companies. He summarized everything by saying that "I must never disappoint my beloved parents". After all the discussions, everybody went to bed.

The following morning, Okoro and Uluma accompanied Uche toMr. Nwogu's house where they were received warmly. Before kola was served, Mr. Nwogu said "the fly that approaches any animal that has no tail is scared away by the animal's defender who is his creator. It is because Okoro would have found it difficult to train his son in a costly college that his creator had sent for him a helper in the form of scholarship to Uche".

He congratulated Uche for his achievements and thanked Okoro and his wife for their courage, support and steadfastness in sending Uche to school. He mentioned that he will be ready to assist Uche achieve his educational ambition whenever called upon to help. The two couples chatted together on issues of common interests. They ate and drank together before Okoro and his wife departed for their home.

Uche stayed at Nwogu's house before the date of the reopening of his college. For two days, Mr. Nwogu kept telling Chika and Uche of school life, how it looks like, situations that could come up from time to time, and how to make good use of opportunities, time and resources. He, however, warned the boys to desist from voracious eating. "You don't because food is sweet, you eat too much of it which may affect your studies and physical wellbeing", Mr. Nwogu toned. He advised them on how to make use of his initiatives to overcome adverse situations.

Mr. Nwogu sternly advised Chika and Uche to take their studies seriously and to refrain from acts of indiscipline. Mr. Nwogu promised to be visiting Uche and Chika at intervals; when occasion calls for that.

When the day for the reopening of the school came, Mr. Nwogu accompanied Uche and Chika to their school.

They reported first tothe principal, who immediately recognisedthem.

The principal congratulated the young men for their success even though Uche was nearly robbed of it. The principal emphasized the need for truth and honesty in the public and private life and advised the boys to be reliable and honest in all their dealings in the school if theywant to live happilyin the school.

After the advice, the principal gave the boys the necessary forms to fill, before he finally admitted them into class 1 of the school. He later allocated them to different hostels.

The following day, the boys copied the time table forstudies and other activities. The boys never disobeyed theregulations. They always did their assignments regularly. Within ten days, the boys had mastered the regulations and always adhered to them without being instructed to do so. The school was a large sized one and as such labour was demandedfrom the students to help keep the College in a good state. So,manual work was done occasionally.

CHAPTER EIGHT

One afternoon, when everybody was busy doing his normal work, a boy in form two called on Uche. Uche quickly responded. He ran to the boy obediently thinking that the boy had called him for something reasonable, Uche did not know that he was going to get something different. As Uche approached the boy, the boy immediately rebuked Uche, saying "you toad, what is your toad number. Who even brought you into this school. You black goose. Speak to me, you idle monkey".

As Uche was about opening his mouth to ask what was happening, the boy closed his mouth claiming that Uche's mouth was smelling. Remembering what he was told not to fight, Uche immediately left the scene. As he was going away, the boy quickly called Uche back but Uche kept a deaf ear on him. The boy was angry and imiediately ran to Uche and drew Uche back. Uche quickly removed the boy's hand from him and went on. The boy drew Uche back again and Uche's anger was aroused. Uche gave the boy a slap and ran away. That happened within a twinkle of an eye.

Everybody was surprised; even Uche's class mates. When some students discovered what has happened they made a hot chase to catch Uche. Uche ran as he never did before, straight to the principal's house and into the man's parlourwhere the man was relaxing reading his European Journal. "Good afternoon sir" Uche greeted. The man responded thus, "good afternoon". "A student is chasing me Sir and I have come to you for rescue", Uche said. The Principal quickly got up from his chair to see what was happening.

While coming outside his parlour the principal saw Uche's opponent OfeOduwhile other students with him had deserted him. "What has gone wrong?" the Principal asked the young man. When the two people made their statements, the principal asked them to go to the Disciplinary Master who will handle the case. He dropped a note to be given to the Disciplinary Master through Uche. In the letter, the Principal requested the master to judge the case and recommend disciplinary measures on the offender to him. The two boys left for the Disciplinary Master's house.

During the interrogation, Uche was first allowed to explain what happened. He laid the facts from start to the end. His opponent was later given a chance. He lied at the middle of the explanation by denying that he said that Uche's mouth wassmelling. A witness was called who confirmed the assault. After the interrogations, the Disciplinary Master wrote a summary of what happened and recommended disciplinary actions to be taken by the Principal.

In the paper, the teacher condemned OfeOdu for raining abuses on Uche and forlieing. He, however, frowned at Uche for taking the law into his hands by slapping his senior, but mentioned that it was an act of provocation. However, the Disciplinary Master recommended that Odu be suspended for two weeks from the institution to act as a deterrent to other students who may have the intention to assault other students. He recommendedthat Uche be sternly warned to desist from fighting.

After going through the paper, the Principal approved all the recommendations. The following day, the Principal called up Uche Okoro and OfeOduto the assembly. He frowned at the fighting and warned that the school willhenceforth not condone any act of lawlessness. He preached peace. He announced two weeks suspension of Odu first. After that, he warned Uche claiming that he was lenient with him because he was a new comer.

Before the assembly came to an end, the principal reiterated the need for the students to live peacefully together. He advised the old students to take their new ones as their younger ones and not to treat them as strangers. He, however, stressed that he will not tolerate any act of lawlessness from any student again; be it an old student or a new one no matter the circumstance.

CHAPTER NINE

While in the school, Uche grew from strength to strength. He made great achievements in academics, sports and in the social life of the school.In his first and second term results in his first year, he performed creditably well and had the second and first positions respectively in a class of fifty two students. His achievements at school flew like missiles in the air and stormed his village every now and then.

Uche loved arts but performed better in the sciences. He loved stories a lot and told a lot of them. But Uche was very good in calculations, experimentations and scientific practicals. In fact, he was all around in the academic system. He was very illustrious.

During the third term of Uche's first year in school, the Senior Prefect of the school announced that the fresh students of the session would be integrated fully into the school system in a programme known as "cutting tale".

In the evening of that sunday, the old students rejoiced because it was a programme in which they show theirsuperiority over the new ones. An adage goes that "whatever someone does not know is greater than the person". Uche, not familiar with the programme, kept his mouth shut over it. Some of the new students were however happy for they thought it would be to their advantage.

That evening after meals, which the old students knewwas the timefor the exercise, every place was strengthened with security till the Senior Prefect and some other school functionaries arrived for the activity. When theyarrived, they were applauded.

Thereafter, the Senior prefect asked the fresh students to kneel down, which they did immediately. The Senior Prefect advised the new students on the need for proper education, hardwork, obedience, neatness, love, tolerance among other good things. He advised them to sit up to their responsibilities if they want to stay happilyin the school.

Later the Senior Prefect asked the students to stand up. He further asked the Disciplinary Prefect to flog each andevery new student a light stroke of the cane. That was done quietly. That according to the Senior Prefect is to make the new students sit up to their responsibilities as some of them have not been up and doing in their responsibilities. The Senior Prefect further said that, that is how canes pain for those who may derail and wish to be flogged and advised the new students to always do the right thing at the right time. Thereafter the Senior Prefect and other school functionaries left the place.

Before the students went in to read that night, some old students took their turn of the exercise. They marched out the new students in front of the refectory and commanded them to march about twelve metres on their knees. When all the new boys had obeyed them, they flogged each and every one of the new studentsfive strokes of the cane. After that, they asked the new ones tolie on the floor for ten minutes, after which they went to read.

Uche was greatly annoyed. He did not read,or sleep that night. Finally he concluded that he will travel the following morning.

The following morning, Uche took permission and left the school for Mr. Nwogu's house far away from the school. There, Uche explained everything that happened to him to Mr. Nwogu. The man sympathized with Uche and promised to lead him to the principal to speak on his behalf.

Mr. Nwogu led Uche to the Principal. When they came to the principal, Mr. Nwogutold the principal what happened to Uche and his colleagues. The principal was surprised and could not believe it. He immediately sent for those who carried out the operation. He gathered the school at the assembly ground immediately and announced the immediate suspension of the five leaders of the operation. He suspended them for aweek. Privately he warned Uche not to take matters within the school outside without first informing him. With that, Uche learnt a crucial thing pertaining the school.

CHAPTER TEN

Later, the third term came to an end. During the long vacation, Uche spent three quarter of the vacation period in Mr. Nwogu's house. He helped the man on his farms, and in domestic work. He also spent some of his time teaching students at the village school with Mr. Nwogu.

With Uche at Mr. Nwogu's house during the holiday were two girls. One was theyounger sister to Mrs. Nwogu while the other was the daughter of Mr. Nwogu's sister. All were spending the long vacation withMr. Nwogu and his family.

On one market day, Uche accompanied Mrs. Nwogu to the market along withthe two girls. Mrs. Nwogu bought many food items in three baskets. When it was time to go home, the girls hurriedly carried the smaller baskets leaving the big one for Uche. Uche seeing that it was histurn decided to do justice to the big basket. He tried to lift it butit was too heavy for him. Mrs. Nwogu went to help him. Theysucceeded in lifting it up to Uche's head.

Mrs. Nwogu asked Uche whether the load was too heavy for him, but Uche replied "no". Uche was onlypretending. The two girls cajoled Uche by saying "are you not a man?" Uche replied "why not". The load was too heavy for Uche but he pretended as if nothing was wrong. He kept smiling but suffering in silence.

The weight of the load kept shouldering on Uche that it eventually went off his head and fell down. Uche looked helpless and was extremely annoyed. On seeing his face changing, the two girls kept their peace. Uche only sat on a wooden tree to rest.

On recovering from his lost fatigue, Uche picked his rag and went away. Uche should have told the girls that the load was too heavy for him but he wanted to keep to his words of being a man. He was trying to showcase his strength. On getting home the girls relayed the news to Mr.Nwogu and his wife who had earlier returned home.

Mr. Nwogu sympathized with Uche while his wife directed that Uche should not be assigned such a difficult task again. Immediately, other people went for the basket and brought it back.

CHAPTER ELEVEN

After the long vacation, Uche and Mr. Nwogu's son Chika packed to their school. As said earlier, the two boys looked alike, played much with oneanother, possessed similar characters and behavedalike. In fact, some people believed that they were twins, or children from the same mother. As the new academic session progressed, the two boys tried to sail above board. They never missed classes. They adhered to the school rules and regulations and gave academics the priority it deserves.

One morning, the first lesson to be taught in Uche's class was English language. The subject master was aEuropean, Mr. Blank, a tall, handsome well-behaved gentleman. That white man always kept to time. Before it was time for the English lesson, Mr. Blank was already inside the class. On seeing the teacher, the class monitor beat the locker and the students greeted "good morning Sir". The teacher responded "goodmorning ladies and gentlemen". The teacher immediately said "sorry for including ladies, since there are no ladies here".

One of the students rose up and asked the teacher if there was any other way of excluding ladies during greetings since the words ladies goes with gentlemen. The teacher asked if any student can help with the question. Uche raised his hand up and was granted permission. Uche said that the only way of saying ladies and gentlemen is by saying "ladies and jerrymen" Everybody burst into laughter and Uche was nicknamed "jerrymen". That was how Uche came to be called jerrymen, a nickname which he bore throughout his stay at the college.

Initially, Uche opposed the name by refusing to respond to it but after a short while he accepted it, wholeheartedly. Throughout the remaining part of his stay at the college, Uche's nickname "jerrymen" echoed round the four corners of the college and beyond.

In his early days in the college, Uche spent a good time in the laboratories watching the senior students doing their practical works. At a time he watched them study the oscillation of a pendulum. Uche further admired how the students prepared their soap and how they spent their good times doing one thing or the other at the laboratories. He loved when preserved animals are used at the laboratories and had sacrificed some of his time hunting for some to be kept at the laboratories. In fact, Jerrymen (Uche) was good in sciences. He loved doing practical works at the laboratories and as a result devoted time and interest in sciences.

When Mr. Nwogu came to see Chika and Uche, he came to the school gate and met the gatemen. He informed

A Way Forward

the men that he wanted to see his son and Uche. When the gatemen asked one of the students to help call Uche, the student replied "is it Uche the Jerry" The gatemen and Mr. Nwogu were surprised. When Mr. Nwogu described Uche and mentioned his surname the student came to be sure of the Uche Mr. Nwogu meant - Uche the Jerry. Later Chika and Uche were called out for Mr. Nwogu.

When Uche was called out, Mr. Nwogu asked him how he came about the nickname Jerrymen. Uche relayed theinformation to Mr.Nwogu from start to end. Mr. Nwogu said that he will examine the nickname and promised to discipline Uche if he chose to answer the name for moral laxity. Mr. Nwoguprivately asked Chika how Uche came about the nickname Jerry. When Chika relayed the message it was similar to Uche's own. Hearing the same story, Mr. Nwogu ignored the nickname.

In those days, suits were highly regarded and those who wore suits were highly respected. Uche being a lover of good things had his eyes set forth for a day he would have a pair of suit to himself.

Then, there was a student whose father was a dealer insuits. Some students who wanted suits bought such through the student, who later gave the money to the father.

At the end of the third term, the school organises a send-off for the graduants. After the occasion, people were allowed to put on mofty clothes. That gave the students who had the scarce suits to have them on.

So, as Uche was going home for the long vacation, he made up his mind to purchase a pair of suits for himself. He gave the issue a serious thought. In the interim, he realized that to have a suit is a privilege and not a right. As such, his father may not grant the request. Moreover, his father may see it as a luxury and frown at it.

When Uche thought over the matter a solution came to him. He planned a deal. He planned to frame a lie and tellhis father that he has broken an item at the laboratory for which he had been surcharged. When Uche woke up one morning, hewent to his father and told him that he was doing some practical work at the laboratory one day and accidentally a thermometer went off his hands and broke on the floor. Hementioned that as a result, some of his belongings were seized by the school authority. He claimed that he would have been suspended for some weeks if the authority had not known him to be a good boy. He said all that in a very sober mood for sympathy.

His father was greatly afraid "ta-mo-mi-ta" Okoro beckoned. "What is it all about", Okoro asked. "It is just a laboratory equipment imported from overseas for laboratory work" Uche replied. "But if it is replaced can the school mete any other punishment on you?" Okoro asked. "No" Uche replied. "What is the cost?" Okoro questioned. "Two pounds" Uche replied. Okoro presumed that his son had been a good boy and would not intentionally commit a crime.

Okoro was determined to do anything for his boy's educational welfare. He rushed inside his house, brought out two pounds and one shilling and gave it to his son. He asked Uche to rush to the school immediately, pay themoney and collect his seized items and come back for hisholiday. Okoro did not take chance as one adage says that "a weed is better removed when small because if it develops a good root system, it may prove difficult to pull out". That is to say that, it is good to resolve a matter when it is fresh than when it has developed properly.

Uche quickly took the money, prepared immediately and left. He did not go to the school but rather went to a neighbouring village where he visited a friend. He wasted three days there, before he came back. When he came, he quickly hid the money inside hiswooden box and waited for his father to come back. When Okoro came back, Uche told him that he had paid the money and as such has resolved the matter. He had kept the suit money in his box waiting for the reopening of the school when the suit dealer would come.

When the school reopened after the long vacation, Uche waited for the suit dealer to negotiate for one. When the man came, Uche looked round the heaps of suits and finally selected a blue one. Bearing in mind the cost, Uche brought out two pounds from his pocket and gave the seller. The seller counted the money and in turn told Uche that it remains two shillings. Uche was surprised. "But you have been selling this item for two pounds, isn't it?" Uche asked. "Yes" the man responded. "But why is my own an exception" Uche asked dizzily. The man said that there was an increase in the price by the wholesalers. Uche took back his money and went back to the hostel.

As he was going away, he battled with his mind whether to add the two shillings and buy the suit or not. As he went into the hostel, he kept thinking over the matter until he finally came to a point. The point was that he remembered the importance of the item to him and concluded that he would add some money and buy the item.

Before he came to the school, his father had given him three shillings, his mother a shilling while Mr. Nwogu gave him another shilling. That totaled five shillings. Out of this money, he had used one and half shilling to buy some of his educational needs like pens, exercise books and ink leaving him with three and half shillings. For him to utilize two shillings out of the three and half shillings remaining to buy the suit will pose for him a serious financial problem.

But considering the importance of the suit to him, he had to succumb. He went inside his wooden box, brought out two shillings from it and set out to the suit arena. When he reached there, he brought out the suit money and gave it to the seller and collected the suit. After purchasing the suit, Uche found it difficult to meet up with his needs as he was left with only one and half shilling.

After about a week of the suit business, a lot of financial incurrence came in, his bathroom slippers had torn, he needed to repair it, he had to buy more soap for domestic operations and he needed some money for miscellaneous expenses. One and half shilling would not be enough for all that.

When Uche laid his financial problem to one of his friends, the friend simply replied "that's a little problem. I will give you a quick solution". Uche's friend told him to go to his parents and tell them that the school had levied three shillings for examination, one shilling for send-off of outgoing students and one shilling for a science textbook.

The boy told Uche to be frowning and to be serious while saying such. That according to Modubere, Uche's friend will make it possible for his parents to take the matter serious and expedite action in giving him the money. Uche hearkened to Modubere and went home to do what he learnt. He succeeded. Uche had lied. When Uche had succeeded he nicknamed his suit "Uche's deal". He later wrote the word "Uche's deal" on the suit's collar. That was because of the financial mess the suit put him, and how he tried to overcome the problem through telling lies.

During the third term of his fourth year in the college, Uche was nominated along with two other students for election into house prefectship of the hostel. The house prefectship was decided by majority vote among the house occupants. Any nominee that received the highest vote count was regarded as the chosen one. Uche the popular young man known as Jerry or Jerrymenworked very hard for the election.

Two days was granted for canvassing ofvotes. Uche spent those nights and the days canvassing for votes. Jerry was more popular among the students than the other two contestants. His nickname Jerrymen or Jerry made him very popular.

At the election, Uche had a landslide victory. Nevertheless, the election cost him thingsranging from food, gifts to books amongother things including giving money to students to vote for him. Uche hada book which he read during his second year, but which he used for reference in his fourth year. During the campaign, he gave it to a student at the second year to get his vote. After the election, Uche found out that he was still going to use the book. He went to the student he had given it to, to collect it back. The boy refused. Uche was annoyed and he fought the boy and wounded him.

The boy reported the matter to the House Master who referred the case to the Disciplinary Master. The Disciplinary Master looked into the case and gave the Principal his recommendations. He recommended that Uche should be relieved of his post for using resources to canvass for votes and in addition go on two weeks' suspension. The recommendation was accepted and the following morning it was implemented.

Uche was asked to relinquish his position for the first runner up in their election and proceed on two weeks' suspension. Immediately his property was brought out across the gate by the school warders. When Uche got home on suspension, he told his parents that he was on a brief holiday to enable him settle and prepare for the school examinations.

After the suspension, Uche packed and came back to the school. When he came back, he became a changed person. An adage says that "you don't need to tell a deaf man that the market is in chaos". He never did "what can bring two legs into a trouser". He read seriously for the term's examinations. He desisted from any bad act. He became a respecter of the law and the school authority.

A Way Forward

It should be further noted that Okoro had four children after Uche - two sons and two daughters. Later on, Okoro's first daughter grew up to the age of attending school. Okoro contemplated sending the girl to school to learn and also be an asset to him. But along the line he relinquished the idea. Thereason was that the husband will be the beneficiary of her education, which he (Okoro) provided with his hard-earned money, when she grows up and eventually marries.

With that notion, Okoro abandoned the idea of sending his first daughter to school. That was one of the reasons for the very poor educational state of women in Umuele and her environs in those uncivilized days.

CHAPTER TWELVE

Later, Uche enrolled for the London School Certificate Examination with others in his fifth year. After a short time, the examination came up and Uche did his best at it. During one of the examinations, Uche saw a boy copying somebody's work. The boy succeeded in the dirty act. The boy was not caught. Uche concluded that he will practise that dirty game during the nextpaper. Before the paper came up, Uche copied something on a paper which he thought would be one of the questions in the examination.

Before the paper was taken, the invigilator announced that whoever had anything unwanted in the examination hall should please take it outside. On hearing that, Uche's mind shook. He was greatly afraid. And as destiny is not the same with everybody, Uche went out and removed the material because of fear.

Immediately, he came in, the invigilator conducted a search on the inner pockets of all the students. Uche had earlier kept the unwanted material inside his front pocket. When hewas searched he was happy that he had removed the material which would have implicated him.

When the question paper was distributed, Uche discovered that what he copied did not even appear among the questionsto be answered.

Before the examination result came out (which was marked in London) Uche engaged in a teaching job in his home town in anew mission primary school. He was paid four shillings a month. Uche attended work from his house; otherwise he would have lived from hand to mouth. The salary was not enough for him but he tried to make both ends meet since he was going to work from his home and was under the control and care of his parents.

While on the teaching job, Uche realized that it was the meager salary that some salary earners earn that make some of them use tape to measure the yam they cook for food.

After about two months in his hometown, Uche was transferred to a neighbouring school. The distance of that school from his hometown was a bit long and Uche decided to live in the school. Before Uche packed to his new station, his mother had bought him utensils which he took with him to his new station. He used the little money he saved at work to buy variety of clothes. He also bought another pair of suits. He made sure he puton the latest dress in the fashion list. He had a friend who supplied him with the latest designs in clothing.

As Uche assumed duties at Umuzu, his new station, he grew from strength to strength. While at Umuzu village school, he was given a comfortable accommodation at the school's staff quarter. His house had two rooms.

One day, while at the school, one of his neighbours, a teacher too, asked Uche to accompany him to his village

Epele for their annual yam festival. Uche obliged and accompanied his neighbour home for the occasion. That is proper since "the sheep believes that there is nothing as good as seeing things physically". Also, the event was on a Sunday and as such a work free day at the mission school.

At Epele, Uche's neighbour by name Efor entertained Uche very well with food and drinks at his family compound. After that, Uche and Efor left for the village's rendezvous to grace the entertainment activities which marked the annual event.

At the square where the event took place properly, activities of different sorts were there. There was masquerade displays and cultural and traditional dances by different people and different groups.

As the masquerades performed, Uche and his friend watched them from different angles as it is believed that "masquerade are better watched from different positions".

There was a lady from the town who came to greet Uche and his colleague. After greeting the two young men, the lady asked Mr. Efor whohis colleague was. Mr. Efor replied that the person was a fellow teacher, Mr. Uche Okoro who had sacrificed his time to accompany him to this great occasion. The lady requested to know more about Uche. Uche accepted. The two came out at a lonely place, discussed issues and exchanged addresses. Uche felt shy.

The lady,Ngozo, promised to relate with Uche soon. Uche had not had such an experience before. Uche and his colleague came back to their station that Sunday evening.

A week later, Efor visited his home where he saw Ngozo. Ngozo used that opportunity to write to Uche. The lady was sound in education and as a matter of fact was schooling in a Girls' College. The letter was written thus:

>Mount Camel College,
>Anyaudu.
>13th March.
>
>Sweet Heart,
>
>I hope you are fine in health. I hope you can recall when we met at our festival. My name is NgozoNolu. I quite admire you both physically and otherwise. I really love you and will like to relate with you. I will even like to marry you if you accept my desire. The way you behave, walk, talk and speak are all interesting to me. You are the type of man I like and if you accept what I have requested from you, you will not regret it.
>
>   Give the reply to Efor when he is coming back or you can post the letter to me with the above address. I hope to hear favourably from you. Bye bye.
>
>>Your Sweet Heart,
>>NgozoNolu (Miss)

This lady had written this same letter with her village address. But remembering that she may be in the school when the reply may come, she rewrote the same letter with another sheet of paper and with another envelop.

This lady was a fiancée to one man, a carpenter. The man had been sponsoring Ngozo in her school and actually wanted to marry her. But Ngozo did not like to marry the man considering his poor educational background. Ngozo was looking for another person to marry and replace that her fiancée, the illiterate. Ngozo has seen Koko as someone who is mentally and intellectually below her capacities and the thought has given her sleepless nights. When Ngozo gave Uche's letter to Mr. Efor, she left for school.

But when Ngozo's fiancé, the carpenter came to her house, he saw the abandoned letter. The man being an illiterate could not read the letter. He invited a pupil schooling in a primary school to read the letter for him. When the boy had finished reading the letter to him, the carpenter was annoyed. Ngozo had not been responding to his marriage proposal and he thought that somebody must be the brain behind that.

The carpenter enquired about Uche's address. The person that read the letter told him. Koko, boiling with anger, quickly set off for Umuzu Community School to meet Uche and possibly deal with him for confusing and spoiling his fiancée.

When Koko got to Uche's house, he entered his room without knocking. He sat down later. The man acting foolishly neither greeted Uche nor made any enquiries when he saw Uche. He rather asked Uche why he had decided to deceive, spoil, romance and confuse his fiancée Ngozo. From the look of things, the man was out to deal with any person making it difficult for Ngozo to respond favourably to his marriage proposal and for him to win her heart completely.

Uche was extremely surprised. He did not know what to do. He went out to invite Efor and others to come and see what was happening. When Efor and another teacher came in, they tried to intervene but Uche asked the carpenter, Koko to go out of his house. Uche tried to push him out and in the process the two young men fought. Efor ran to get the police who came immediately and arrested the carpenter and took him to the police station. At the police station the police made peace between the warring parties.

After that, Uche wrote to Ngozo disagreeing with her request. The letter was written thus:

> Umuzu School
> 4th, April
>
> Dear NgozoNolu,
>
> I don't like how your friend or fiancée embarrassed me in my house because of you. I may run into more problems in future if I relate with you. So, I don't want to relate with you.

> Whoever is not careful of ladies may die carelessly. I am careful and want to live long.
>
> Thank you and bye bye.
> Uche Okoro

Ngozo felt very unhappy when she read Uche's letter. She wept also. The shock lasted for sometime.

With that unpleasant and unpalatable letter, Ngozo's desire to relate intimately with Uche could not hold. She got married to Koko eventually.

Two weeks later, the School Certificate result was released. Uche made the best result in his school. He performed wonderfully in the science subjects. In addition, he was awarded a scholarship by the British Government for making the best result in the school and also for making the best result in the sciences. The scholarship was tenable in the United Kingdom witha duration of first degree minimum and a master's degree maximum.

In the scholarship letter, which was accompanied with the result, Uche was requested to report to the British National Office to complete the necessary formalities within two weeks otherwise the offer would lapse. When Uche saw the result with the scholarship, he quickly collected them, discussed same with the school principal and rushed home. The principal promised to bear part of the cost of his travelling expenses to and fro Lagos where the British National Office was situated.

Uche took the result and the scholarship letter to Mr. Nwogu; thereafter to his parents. There was jubilation all the way. He collected the necessary documents required by the British Governor, like Standard Six Leaving Certificate result remaining the letter from a respected citizen testifying of his good character and Medical Fitness Certificate attesting to his good health.

HisPrincipal issued him his school testimonial and wrote for him a letter testifying of his good character. The following morning, Uche rushed for a Medical Certificate at the District Hospital. He was examined and he succeeded in getting it. The following day, he planned his trip to Lagos.

Two days later, Uche left for the British Office inLagos for this scholarship affair. He was accompanied byMr. Nwogu. Mr. Nwogu has been immensely impressed with Uche's performances and had always liked to associate with him.Such is normal as an adage says that "the eye always focuseson good things".

Before they left for Lagos, Uche had his bath in Mr. Nwogu's house that morning. When Mr. Nwogu was going to have his, he perched his legs on some banana peel which was lying on the floor and fell down accidentally and had some injuries. His wife was annoyed and queried bitterly thus, "is Uche your son that you are suffering for him like that. Is he your relation either? What relationshiphave you with him?"

She immediately ran to Uche to lay her grievance, "I think you have gotten your own parents to take care of you and your problems. Why have you decided to bring your problems to Nwogu for solution. Look at what hashappened to him. For goodness sake, please leave my house and go home before my anger falls on you" the woman said.

Uche not being the cause of Nwogu's problem and not expecting such statements from Mrs. Nwogu whom he knew very well as a good woman became extremely surprised. He made some comments to Mrs. Nwogu as words of appeal. But that looked like water poured on a stone. Mrs. Nwogu kept on uttering some carefree words to Uche who later left the area for his home.

On his way home, Mr. Nwogu called Uche back. Hegave Uche some words of advice and asked him to forget all the words his wife had uttered. Uche was surprised at the situation but nevertheless relaxed. He realised the adage which says that "it is good for the air to blow so that everybody can see the true physical appearance of the fowl". That is to say that it is good for people to be at times in difficulty to see how some people will react towards them. However, Uche learnt from the incident not to trust people completely and to be careful withhuman beings.

After the incidence, Mr. Nwogu prepared and left for Lagos with Uche. They boarded an open lorry to Lagos, which took themabout two days to accomplish the journey. Mr. Nwogu incurred all their expenses feeding,transport fare among other expenses for thejourney, even though Uche's Principal made a little provision for that.

When they got to Lagos, they boarded another lorry to the British National Office. There, they presented their invitation letter and were allowed inside the reception. They met the secretary to the British Office who congratulated Uche and directed him to prepare for his studies in Britain. After filling all the necessary documents, the secretary told them that the scholarship was only tenable in Great Britain and that it was in recognition of Uche' s brilliant performance in his school final examinations more especially in the sciences. He asked Uche to go home and prepare within three weeks for his trip within a month.

When Uche got home, he broke the news. There was jubilation all over. Mr. Nwogu told Okoro Oba that the best is yet to come fromUche. Within the little time granted them, Uche prepared heavily for his trip overseas.

A big send off was organisedfor Ucheby the entire Umuele community. During the send-off ceremony, everybody advised Uche to be careful with women and in all his dealings in Britain. During the send-off which lasted almost a day, the foremost to speak was the eldest man in the village. He told Uche that whoever much is given much is expected of him. He said that Uche's nuts have been cracked for him by nature so that he can bring relief to their community by employing white man's developmental ideas to their community. He advised Uche to be careful and desist from acts that could bring disgrace to their community. He advised Uche not to marry a white woman who may not know their culture, language, tradition and values.

The discussion, which focused on similar issueslike honesty, carefulness and not marrying a white lady, was rounded offwith various traditional dances and plays. After the occasion, gifts ranging from money to foods came generously to Uche.

In the night, Okoro told Uche the old stories of his youth where he lost many things because of his illiteracy which only came at Uche's advantage. He told Uche the benefits of good education. He later told Uche to be very careful in Britain where he was going for further studies. He said, "my son, if you are going out for food, I shouldn't have let you out because I have excess of it. If it is for fun or any sort of enjoyment I can satisfy you with that. Even if it means selling all my assets and marrying for you as many wives as you like or giving you any material thing, I can satisfy you. You wouldn't have left me. Please, remember home. Yourperson is very important to us. I should have asked you to stay with us and refuse your scholarship award but for the fact that you are going for good, I will let you go. Remember that 'whoever his house is on fire does not hunt for mice'. Remember that you are the pillar of my house and when the pillar of a house goes off or is weak the house is bound to fall".

Later, a collective prayer was said for Uche's good intentions. Uche in his response promised to remain the good Uche he is. He promised to be of good character throughout his stay in Britain. He promised to be writing his people all the time. He said that to take proper care of home will always inhis mind. When all parties have heard from one another, it was concluded that "fine birds have made fine feathers". Thereafter, all parties left one another.

The following day, Uche set out for Lagos this time in the midst of many. They included his father, Mr. Nwogu, his father's half-brother and Uche's colleague in the part time teaching profession, Mr. Efor. They all escorted Uche. They were all received at the British Office. They stayed there, awaiting directives. On the second day, they escorted Uche to the wharf where he boarded the ship for the Britain trip.

CHAPTER THIRTEEN

Uche stayed twenty days on sea before he got to Britain. When he got there, he presented his travel documents to the relevant authorities before he was driven to the Uptown University where he was given admission. He was comfortably accommodated at the school.

The university was a big one with amenities and infrastructure. Uche registered formally into the school. He was in the College of Medicine. At the University, Uche was given the University's regulations contained in a booklet. He was on a British Government Scholarship and practically lacked nothing. He stayed a week before the school reopened after the vacation. When the school reopened, Uche copied his time table and was anxious to learn.

Among his mates, Uche was the only black man. On the first day he went for his lesson, he had a bitter lesson. On seeing Uche, some of his other colleagues took to their heels. They kept him isolated. Many of them closed their nose with their fingers and went away. Some made mockery of him. Uche was completely surprised and disillusioned.

Bitterly, Uche went to a lecturer to ask if anything had gone wrong. But the lecturer said that there was no cause for alarm. Still, most of the students were shouting and mocking him. Uche's anger broke and he took his paper and pen and went away.

In his absence, the lecturer called back the students to instruct them not to isolate Uche but many paid deaf ears and did not come back. When Uche went to his residence, he was deep in thought. He thought of his bitter experience, over and over but could not find an answer. Uche could not swallow that. He left for the office of the Provost of the College to express his bitter experience to him. On hearing the story, and the Provost being aware of such treatments to blacks accepted to look into the case. The man privately advised the white students to accept the black young man as a colleague.

After sometime, Uche started having some white friends (both sexes) and started associating with them. But some of them were still unfriendly and unaccomodating. So, Uche was careful in his relationship with people. Some white people in the University still saw Uche as a sub-standard human being who could be compared or equivalent to an advanced monkey and treated him as such.

During his first year in the university, Uche had started attending parties along with his white counterparts. Uche had seen the light. He had seen fun. Uche who came from a timid background thought that he had lost a lot of fun in his life time. So, he overdid certain things.

In fact, Uche used most of his time attending parties and other forms of occasions with his white counterparts. Like an adage says "you cannot use two legs at the same time while crossing a river". So, Uche's academic work suffered as a result of his excessive involvement in occasions and parties. Uche failed that first term. The BritishGovernment in Lagos, his home country had already directed some agents in London to be monitoring Uche's life at the college.

So, Uche's recent behaviour like other things done under the sun was known. When the report of his character came to the British Government and a copy of his terminalresult which was bad came as well, the office wrote a reprimand letter to Uche. In the letter, they cautioned Uche to desist from carefree acts otherwise, he would receive a severe disciplinary action.

Uche did not totally desist from those acts but rather indulged in them with style. He only attended night parties and none in the day for fear of being very much noticed. Like the law of nemesis, which pays back everybody his wrong doing, Uche afterall failed the second term examination again. When a copy of his result and the remarks of his character came to the British Office in Lagos, they gave Uche the final warning. They indicated that any other alleged misdemeanor reported of him will attract withdrawal of his sponsorship.

Uche continued in his poor character and had a bad result at the third term. When the British Government heard of his continued acts of indiscipline and saw his bad examination results, they withdrew their sponsorship on

Uche. They wrote a letter to Uche on that and sent a copy of the letter to his school Vice Chancellor and his parents. They further wrote that Uche had been proved to be of very bad conduct. Uche received the letter with shock and fear. He did not know what to do.

In the letter, they requested Uche to train himself at the University or be trained by his parents or withdraw from the school entirely. They wrote that they can only give Uche his ticket fare to board himself and his property from London to Lagos and finally to his home town. Other than that, they said that they have withdrawn any other financial assistance to Uche.

Uche's fee for accommodation, feeding, tuition, books and stationery paid at the beginning of the term by the British Government did not encounter any problem when Uche was on British Scholarship. The money was sent in time. When the term ended and the three weeks holiday was over, the school began the new session.

After about three days, the school authority wrote a letter to Uche demanding his fees for feeding, accommodation and tuition. After about three days with no response from Uche, the school wrote him a reminderin which the school mentioned that if Uche did not pay those fees within seven days he would be withdrawn from the University and be repatriated. When four days passed and it remained three days, Uche ran to his Vice Chancellor for help. The Vice Chancellor used his money to pay for Uche's fees and advised him to write to the British Office in Lagos through him for reconsideration of scholarship. Uche did that immediately.

The Vice Chancellor wrote a covering letter to the British Office recommending Uche for reconsideration. In the reply to the Vice Chancellor's letter which was copied Uche, the British authority accepted Uche's reconsideration ontrial and humanitarian basis. They paid Uche's fees and the Vice-Chancellor took back his money.

From that time onwards, Uche took his studies seriously. He put off attractive activities andconcentrated on his academic work. He performed excellently in all his examinations and was always in good touch with his Vice Chancellor, his good friend. Uche after all, spent seven years for a course which would have had a six year duration. He later specialized in surgery. He worked for about two years in a London hospital.

During Uche's work time, Uche brought in hisimmediate younger brother and Mr. Nwogu's son Chika to the United Kingdom for further studies. He also catered for them before returning home. When Uche returned home, he came in the company of his University Vice Chancellor who wanted to visit Africa for the first time. Uche brought in a car for himself and two motorcycles for his father and for Mr. Nwogu.

When Uche came back, he worked at the Federal Hospital in Lagos. After a month of service at the hospital, Koko, the carpenter who fought Uche in his house because his fiancée wrote a letter to him, brought his son for surgical operation. On seeing Uche Okoro, the man remembered hispast misdeed to him. He hid his face as he discussed with Uche. Uche could not recognize the man anymore.

Like an adage goes that "a sinner runs when nobody is pursuing him". The man was sober. After the surgical operation, the man came to Uche to express himself. After explaining who he was, he begged Uche for forgiveness. Uche asked him not to bear grudges in mind for too long. He, however, emphasized to Koko on the need to be good and to be law abiding. Koko had hidden his face before because he thought that Dr. Uche Okoro would deal with him because of what he did to him many years ago. The men rather ate and drank happily together.

Dr. Uche Okoro returned home and one daywas seen chewing corn.When asked why hepreferred his local food to a foreign one, Dr. Uche stated that he is an African and believes in Africa. He claimed that Africans are superior to the whites just like their food. He claimed that Africa is the symbol of strength, love, peace, development and respect.

Professor J.K. Jopps, the Vice-Chancellor of Uptown University who accompanied Dr. Uche Okoro home stayed about three months with Uche Okoro before returning to London. He maintained a good relationship withDr. Uche Okoro. He visited Dr. Uche Okoro's village among other places of interest in Uche Okoro's country.

Dr. Uche Okoro married six months on his return tohis home country. He married a nurse whom he met at his place of work. He had a successful marriage.

Also, in about eight months of his medical practice at his home country, the person whom Uche fought with at schoolcame for surgical operation. Then, theman OfeOdu by name was very sick and neither Uche nor the patient recognized each other.

Four days after OfeOdu'ssurgical operation, the man regained strength. Then, he recognized whomDr. Uche Okoro was.OfeOdu went to Uche to explain whom he was. On that spot, both parties recognized each other. They talked on a lot of issues which centred on their alma mater, their alumni members among other things. They did nottalk of their quarrel. The two men found out that the world is asmall place where any one is likely to meet another. Again, they ate and drank happily together.

After sometime, Uche appealed the judgement on their land dispute with Jabo at a High court. With overwhelming evidences, he won the land case and took ownership of the plantation proving that the defeat of falsehood over truth is often temporary.

Dr. Uche Okoro influenced the life of many in his community, Umuele in a number of ways. He gave scholarships to deserving students to enable them acquireeducation. People that benefited from the gesture were many and in various levels of education.

Dr. Uche Okoro also assisted in infrastructual development to his community. That was in the provision of portable water, health care services among others. That was the sojourn of Okoro Oba and his son Dr. UcheOkoro. That was "the sojourners" who tried to realize the ambition they wanted through "a right path",the path of hardwork, patience, education, honesty and perseverance – the path of honour and dignity. The way forward

That was how Okoro Oba and Uche Okoro succeeded; by doing the right thing at the right time and at the right place despite the obstacles. That was how the men overcame their challenges and succeeded at the long run.

www.ingramcontent.com/pod-product-compliance
Lightning Source LLC
Chambersburg PA
CBHW030913080526
44589CB00010B/291